Mental Notes

An affirmation and mandala coloring book

©2016 LifeMath Publishing

ISBN 978-0-9863098-2-3

Author + Illustrator: Alexandra Love Sarton

www.alexandra.love

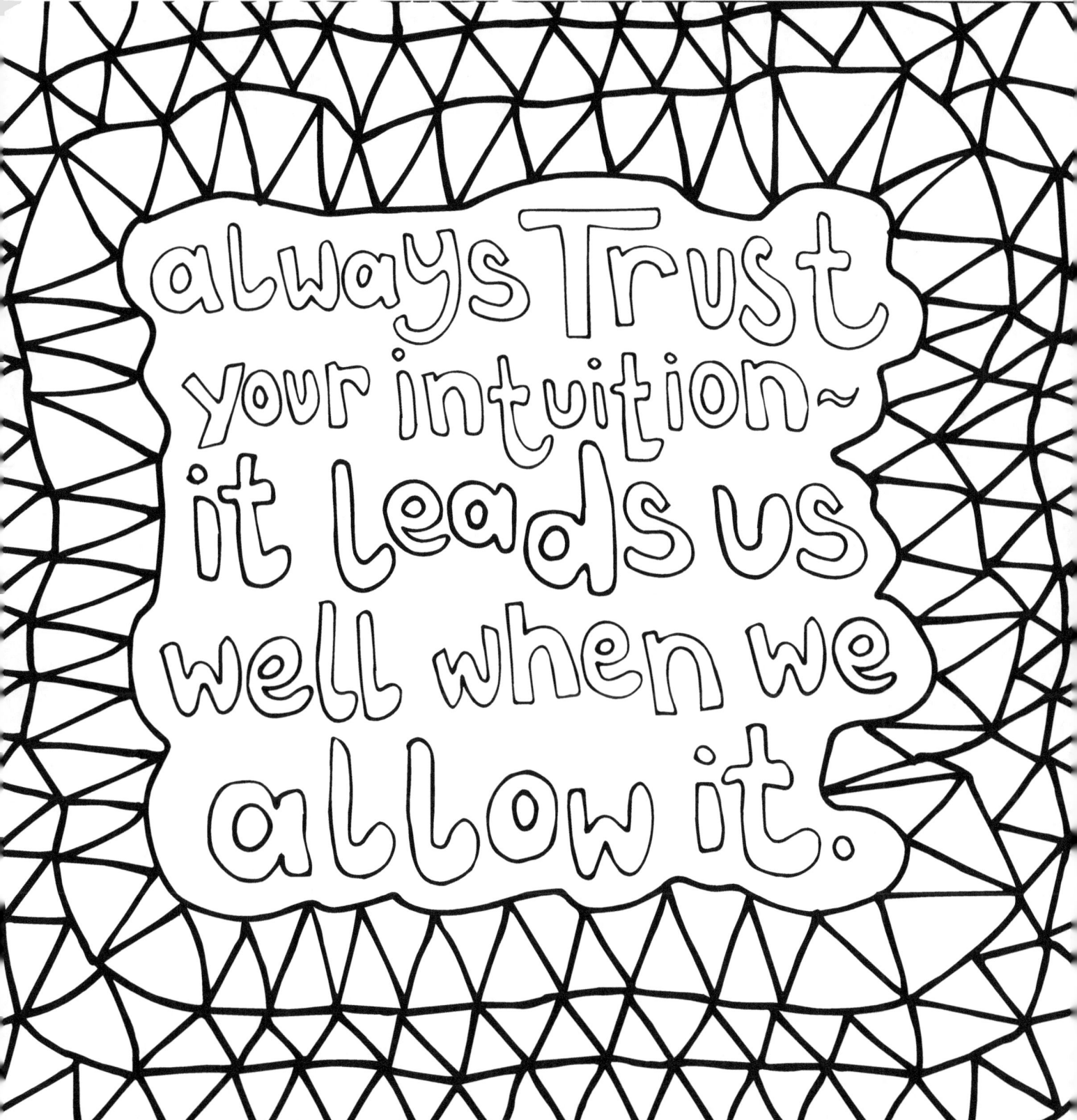

remember to rest. creating time to relax is essential

sit in silence sometimes

talk with the night's stars

take a day to do absolutely nothing

www.ingramcontent.com/pod-product-compliance
Lightning Source LLC
Chambersburg PA
CBHW060516300426
44112CB00017B/2690